MICHELLE KWAN

A Real-Life Reader Biography

John Torres

Mitchell Lane Publishers, Inc.

P.O. Box 619 • Bear, Delaware 19701

Second Printing

Real-Life Reader Biographies

Library of Congress Cataloging-in-Publication Data
Torres, John Albert.
     Michelle Kwan/John Torres.
        p. cm. — (A real-life reader biography)
     Includes index.
     Summary: A biography of the young Chinese-American figure skater who won National and World Championships in 1996 and a silver medal at the 1998 Winter Olympics.
     ISBN 1-883845-97-1 (lib. bdg.)
     1. Kwan, Michelle, 1980- Juvenile literature. 2. Skaters—United States Biography Juvenile literature. [1. Kwan, Michelle, 1980- . 2. Ice skaters. 3. Chinese American Biography. 4. Women Biography.] I. Title. II. Series.
GV850.K93T67 1999
796.91'2'092—dc21
[B]
           99-19933
           CIP

ABOUT THE AUTHOR: John A. Torres is a newspaper reporter for the Poughkeepsie Journal in New York. He has written fourteen sports biographies, including *Greg Maddux* (Lerner), *Hakeem Olajuwon* (Enslow), *Tino Martinez* (Mitchell Lane) and *Darryl Strawberry* (Enslow). He lives in Fishkill, New York with his wife and two children. When not writing, John likes to spend his time fishing, coaching Little League baseball, and spending time with his family.

PHOTO CREDITS: cover: Aubrey Washington/Allsport; p. 4 Jerry Lampen/Archive Photos; p. 11 Mike Powell/Allsport; p. 14 Corbis-Bettmann; p 17 Fred Prouser/ Archive Photos; p. 22 Blake Sell/Archive Photos; p. 24 Jeff Vinnick/Archive Photos; p. 28 Barbara L. Johnston/Archive Photos.

ACKNOWLEDGMENTS: The following story has been thoroughly researched, and to the best of our knowledge, represents a true story. Though we try to authorize every biography that we publish, for various reasons, this is not always possible. This story is neither authorized nor endorsed by Michelle Kwan or any of her representatives.

Table of Contents

Chapter 1
Taking the Ice

Not many people know from a young age what they want to do with their lives. But Michelle Kwan has never been like most other people.

When Michelle was five years old, something happened that would change her life forever. She was at a local ice skating rink with her older sister Karen. They had gone there to see their older brother, Ron, play ice hockey. The girls thought that skating looked like fun. They rented skates and Michelle and Karen took their first steps on the ice.

From the time Michelle was five years old, she knew she wanted to be a skater.

From that moment on, Michelle wanted nothing but to be a world champion figure skater.

Michelle Wing Kwan was born on July 7, 1980, in Torrence, California, a suburb of Los Angeles. Her parents, Danny and Estella Kwan, had both been born in China. Estella was from Hong Kong and Danny was from the Canton area of Mainland China. They met in Hong Kong when they were children, and would marry years later, in 1975, in the United States.

The Kwan family was very close and they helped operate a family business. Estella's parents owned a Chinese restaurant in Torrence called the Golden Pheasant. Estella ran the restaurant as the manager and the children helped out whenever they could.

Michelle was Danny and Estella's third child. When she was born, her family nicknamed her "Little Kwan." Her grandparents gave her a Chinese

When Michelle was born, her family nicknamed her "Little Kwan."

good luck charm. Michelle put it on as a child and never took it off.

Michelle and Karen loved skating all the time. They both were very good on the ice, but Michelle was especially talented. At a very young age she mastered jumps, spins, and turns that are usually difficult for an experienced skater to master.

Michelle also had the perfect attitude to be a great skater. She just wanted to have fun, and did not put a lot of pressure on herself. Her parents were supportive. They just wanted her to have fun, too.

Michelle began competing against other skaters at the age of seven. During one of her first competitions, Michelle fell flat on her face when her name was called. She just laughed, then she went and skated.

It was good for Michelle to have her sister competing with her. They were not only sisters and skating partners, they were also friends.

Michelle and her sister, Karen loved skating all the time. When she was only seven, Michelle entered her first competition.

Danny Kwan made sure that his daughters were not jealous of each other and that they both knew what was important.

"What my wife and I expect from them is not a gold medal, but for them to have a happy life, always," he said.

Chapter 2
Getting Serious About Skating

By the time Michelle was 10 years old, in 1990, she had already won a few tournaments and clearly had championship talent. However, even the most talented skater can not succeed without proper coaching.

Michelle had dreamed of becoming an Olympic champion ever since she watched Brian Boitano win the gold medal at the 1988 Winter Olympics. But training for the Olympics takes a lot of time and costs a lot of money. Skating is a very expensive sport. Danny Kwan had a good job with Pacific Bell

Michelle dreamed of becoming an Olympic champion.

Telephone Company, but the family was by no means wealthy.

To succeed, Michelle and her family would have to dedicate themselves to figure skating. Michelle would have to work very hard and would need a good skating coach. Her parents would have to save their money carefully to pay for the training.

The Kwans decided that both Michelle and Karen should go for it. Michelle was introduced to respected skating coach Frank Carroll. The two liked each other right away. When Michelle started taking lessons from Carroll, she never wanted to take her skates off. She loved to practice, and never complained about the amount of time she was spending on the ice.

In 1991, when Michelle was 11 years old and Karen was 13, their parents decided to move the girls to a figure skating center at Lake Arrowhead, California. The center was a place where serious and famous skaters went to train.

In 1991, Michelle and Karen moved to Lake Arrowhead, California, where serious skaters went to train.

Lake Arrowhead was a new experience for the girls. It was almost like a city of skaters. There was a giant ice skating rink surrounded by mirrors, classrooms, dancing areas, and rooms for the girls to sleep in.

It was the first time in their lives that Michelle and Karen had been away from their parents. They did not have much time to be homesick, though. They were busy all day long with their studies and skating practice. Every

Michelle, left, with sister Karen at Lake Arrowhead, September 1994.

night, Danny Kwan would drive two hours after work to go and see his daughters. A few months later, their mother, Estella, left the restaurant and moved up to Arrowhead to be with the girls all the time.

Every night, Danny Kwan would drive two hours to see his daughters.

Michelle had a lot of natural talent. It was up to her coach to make her a more polished technical skater. He also helped her work on her endurance and strength. Skating competitions include both a short program and a long program. These programs consist of many jumps, flips, and spins. These moves are exciting to watch, but they can be dangerous. If Michelle was not very strong, she could hurt herself during one of her jumps.

When she was 12, Michelle started competing against other top-notch skaters that were about the same age as she was. She began skating in very prestigious competitions for junior skaters. Many people were beginning to notice the little Chinese-American girl with the ponytail.

Michelle won the Southwest Pacific Junior Competition, and placed third in the Pacific Junior Tournament. After such good showings, she was expected to compete for the Junior National Championship in Florida.

For the first time in her life, Michelle got really nervous. She tried too hard and she did not do well. She finished in ninth place.

After it was over, her father reminded her that the important thing was for her to have fun. Michelle put the loss behind her. She was then able to do well in a few other competitions.

In 1993, the top skaters were preparing for the next year's Winter Olympics. Michelle set her sights on the 1994 Games. But the 12-year-old had been competing on the junior level, and junior skaters are not allowed in the Olympics. To qualify, she would have to pass a skating test to reach the senior level.

Michelle's coach wanted her to remain on the junior level for a little

In 1993, Michelle set her sights on the Winter Olympics. To qualify, she had to pass a test to reach the senior level.

longer. He felt that she still had a lot to learn. But Michelle was determined. She took the senior test, and she passed. She was now eligible to compete with the best figure skaters in the world.

In the photo to the right, Michelle skated her long program at the U.S. Figure Skating Championships in January 1993. She finished second in the competition in Detroit, Michigan.

Chapter 3
The 1994 Olympics

As a senior skater, Michelle would have to skate harder and longer. Her parents had to take her out of school and hire a private tutor who would teach around her practice schedule. Michelle missed some of her friends from school, but her closest friends were other skaters at Lake Arrowhead and her sister. Karen had continued skating with Michelle.

Michelle immediately turned heads when she won the Southwest Pacific and Pacific Senior competitions. In 1993, the 12 1/2-year-old competed in the Senior National Championship against

Michelle's closest friends were other skaters from Lake Arrow—head.

such well-known skaters as Nancy Kerrigan and Tonya Harding. Michelle finished in sixth place.

Later that year, Michelle won the Gardiner Trophy in Italy and finished in first place in an Olympic festival in Texas. People were drawn to her energy and her high jumps. Michelle was very comfortable performing in front of people on the ice. She was even named "Skater of the Year" by readers of *Skating Magazine*.

Michelle was still able to enter junior level competitions as well as senior level. In 1994, she won the World Junior Championships. She was getting ready to skate in the most important senior-level competition, the U.S. Figure Skating Championships, when she heard amazing news. Nancy Kerrigan, probably the best skater in the country at that time, was attacked while practicing, and her leg was badly hurt. She would not be able to compete.

The top two finishers in the U.S. Figure Skating Championships would

Michelle is very comfortable performing in front of people on the ice.

go to the 1994 Winter Olympics. As the best American skater, Kerrigan was automatically named to the team. Her rival Tonya Harding edged out Michelle in the competition to gain the second spot on the team.

However, some people thought that Harding had been involved in the attack on Kerrigan. Because of the investigation, Michelle was named as an alternate to the team. She was going to the Olympics!

Michelle accompanied all the other U.S. Olympic athletes to Lillehammer, Norway, for the Games. However, her Olympic

Michelle and coach, Frank Carroll, arrived at the Los Angeles International Airport en route to Norway where Michelle was an alternate skater in the 1994 Winter Olympics.

experience was not that much fun. As an alternate, she was not allowed to compete in the games. She was not allowed to take part in the opening ceremonies, live with the other athletes in the Olympic Village, or even practice with them.

But Michelle was able to watch the other athletes compete and she knew one thing for sure. She would be back in the Olympics, and she would participate.

Nancy Kerrigan came back from her injury to win the silver medal in 1994. A skater from the Ukraine named Oksana Baiul won the gold medal. Although Harding competed, she finished in tenth place.

Shortly after the Olympics, Baiul and Kerrigan became professional skaters. That meant that they could make a lot of money doing shows, but they would be unable to compete in the Olympics again. Harding was banned from amateur competitions when she admitted her involvement in the attack on Kerrigan. As a result, Michelle jumped to the front as America's top-ranked amateur skater.

At the 1994 World Championships, Michelle was the youngest American ever to compete. Michelle's short program was not very good, but she had a brilliant long program. This enabled her to finish in a very respectable eighth place.

In 1995, Michelle was ready for the national championship. By this time, Michelle was already well known throughout the country. She was the spokesperson for the Children's Miracle Network and she was very involved in doing charity work for local pediatric hospitals.

Michelle was in third place after the short program and would have to have an amazing long program if she wanted to finish first. She skated flawlessly and the audience thundered to its feet when she was done. She finished with a second place medal. Her sister did well too, finishing seventh.

Throughout her career, Michelle has been a spokes-person for the Children's Miracle Network and she has been involved in doing other charity work.

Chapter 4
World Champion

As Michelle grew older, she wanted to look more like an adult.

Michelle and her coach, Frank Carroll, were happy with their recent results, but they were not satisfied. They decided to make Michelle's programs even more difficult. Adding more difficult jumps and moves to her routines might make the judges give her higher scores. They also decided to add another person to their team. They hired choreographer Lori Nichol to come up with some new and exciting dance routines for Michelle.

Michelle also decided to show the judges a new look. She cut her hair and wore makeup and costumes that made her look more like an adult. When she showed off her new self at a competition in Detroit, some people did not recognize her right away. However, they knew who she was by the end of the competition, when Michelle won first place.

Near the end of 1995, Michelle was honored by being asked to participate in the tree-lighting ceremony at Rockefeller Center in New York. She skated in front of thousands of admirers before the gigantic Christmas tree was lit. This was a nice break for Michelle, who was anticipating a big year. In just a few months, she would compete in the 1996 U.S. Figure Skating Championship in California. If she did well there, she could compete in the Championship Series Final in France and the World Championship in England.

In her home state of California, Michelle was comforted to have her sister competing with her once again at the 1996 National Championship. Michelle was relaxed and she dazzled

In 1995, Michelle was asked to participate in the tree-lighting ceremony at Rockefeller Center in New York.

onlookers with a tremendous short program and an even better long program. She easily won the competition and became the youngest U.S. champion since 1964. Even though Michelle was a polished skater and practiced very hard every day, she was still only 15 years old.

If people had not heard of Michelle Kwan before, they certainly knew who she was now. Michelle's victory made her a celebrity. She was even able to meet her favorite actor, David Hasselhoff of the television program *Baywatch*.

Her next stop was Paris,

France. Even though Michelle did not skate her best, she totally outclassed her competition and came home with yet another gold medal.

The 1996 World Championship was next. Michelle had a good chance to win. However, she became nervous when a Chinese skater named Chen-Lu gave the performance of a lifetime. Chen-Lu wowed the judges and the crowd. Her performance was so good that she was given two perfect scores of 6.0.

A 6.0 is the highest score you can get in figure skating. Usually a score of 5.7 or 5.8 is considered great. With two perfect scores, Chen-Lu would be hard to beat.

Michelle came out and put herself totally into her routine. She knew that her only chance to win would be to do something really special. She ended her routine by combining two jumps, a triple and a triple toe-loop, one of the toughest skating jumps in the world!

Michelle had a lot of competition at the 1996 World Champion- ship when Chen-Lu received two perfect scores of 6.0.

At the World Figure Skating Championships in March 1996, Michelle and her coach celebrated Michelle's two perfect 6.0 scores.

She added that combination at the last minute in place of an easier jump, and she did it perfectly.

Afterward, Michelle waited breathlessly for her score. She began crying with joy when she was given two perfect scores also! Michelle Kwan won the competition. She had proven that she was the best skater in the world.

"I'm a world champion! I can't believe it," she said. For a while, Michelle even slept with her newest gold medal.

Chapter 5
Going for the Gold

Michelle was the world champion, but her skating expenses were still very high. It was time for her to make some money and pay back her family. She was able to accept money for doing certain skating shows without losing her amateur status. She quickly earned nearly a million dollars.

Even though Michelle was now more secure financially, she remembered how her family had saved to pay for her training. She was very careful with her money. Her favorite clothes were still T-shirts and jeans. As world champion, her life didn't change too much.

As a World Champion, Michelle's life didn't change too much.

Michelle just enjoyed skating and being with her family.

During this time, her sister Karen chose to give up skating full-time and to go to college. She attended Boston University.

In the meantime, the young world champion was feeling the pressure that comes from being on top. Newcomer Tara Lapinski, who had already starred on the junior circuit, was ready to challenge Michelle as another year of competitions began. Both wanted to qualify for the United States' 1998 Olympic team.

When 14-year-old Tara defeated Michelle at the 1997 U.S. championships, Michelle learned how to do something new. She had to be a good loser. The defeated champion gave Tara all the credit in the world for her victory.

Michelle finished a close second to Tara again in the 1997 World Championships. Now she began to worry. Coming in second was a bad thing to start. The 1998 Winter

Olympics, to be held in Nagano, Japan, were next.

Michelle skated beautifully at the Olympics, but she was a little nervous. She was not the same daring skater who had defeated Chen-Lu just a year before. Although her routine was nearly perfect, Lapinski's was even better. Once again Michelle was edged out by the energetic younger skater.

Although Michelle finished in second place, earning an Olympic silver medal, she was so gracious in defeat that she earned even more admiration.

"I think I was a little too overwhelmed by everything," Kwan said. "A year ago, I thought if I don't win, what am I going to do. I thought my life would be over."

Her life was far from over. Although Michelle could have turned professional and earned a lot of money, as Tara Lapinski had after the Olympics, she decided to remain an amateur. She bounced back from the disappointing Olympic defeat to regain her national

At the 1998 Olympics, Michelle earned a silver medal.

and world championship titles in 1998. She also graduated from high school in September, earning a 3.61 grade-point average in the process.

In February 1999, Michelle won the national championship again. It was her third win in four years. Only one other female skater has ever won three

championships. Michelle, though, is hoping that she will have six national titles under her belt by the time the next Winter Olympic Games rolls around in 2002.

In April 1999, Michelle revealed that she would be attending UCLA as a full-time student beginning in the fall of 1999. Michelle says it was a difficult decision for her. "All my life I wanted to go to college and be a student," she said. "A lot of people told me, 'You don't need to go to school. You have enough money.' But that's not what's important. Skating is an important part of my life, but it is only a part. Education is very important to me."

Michelle Kwan has proven that with hard work and commitment, anything is possible. Win or lose, she will always be an inspiration.

Michelle enjoys her skating and only wants to have fun.

Chronology

1980   Michelle is born on July 7
1985   Begins ice skating with sister, Karen
1990   Starts taking lessons from Frank Carroll
1991   Begins training at Lake Arrowhead, California
1993   Places sixth at U.S. championships
1994   Wins World Junior Championships; places second in U.S. Figure Skating Championships; finishes in eighth place at the World Championships
1995   Wins silver medal in the U.S. Championships; comes in fourth place in the World Championships
1996   Caps off a season of victories at the Champions Series Final, Skate America, and Throphee Lalique with gold medals at the U.S. Figure Skating Championships and the World Championships
1997   Wins silver medal in U.S. championships; places second in World Championship
1998   Wins silver medal at the Winter Olympics; wins Gold Medal at the Goodwill Games; wins second national and world championships
1999   Wins third U. S. championship

Michelle's Championships

1999 US Figure Skating Championships—GOLD
1999 Japan Open—GOLD

1998 World Professional Figure Skating Championship—GOLD
1998 The Masters—GOLD
1998 US Professional Figure Skating Classic—GOLD
1998 Keri Lotion Figure Skating Classic—GOLD
1998 Grand Slam—GOLD
1998 Goodwill Games—GOLD
1998 Ultimate Four—GOLD
1998 Hershey's Kisses Skating Challenge (Team)—SILVER

1998 World Figure Skating Championships—GOLD
1998 Winter Olympics—SILVER
1998 US Figure Skating Championships—GOLD

1997 Skate Canada—GOLD
1997 Skate America—GOLD
1997 Nice 'n Easy Figure Skating Classic (team)—SILVER
1997 Hershey's Kisses Skating Challenge (Team)—GOLD
1997 World Figure Skating Championships—SILVER
1997 ISU Champions Series Finals—SILVER
1997 US Figure Skating Championships—SILVER
1997 Honda Prelude Cup—GOLD

1996 Cotton Incorporated Ultimate Four—GOLD
1996 US Figure Skating Postal Service Challenge (Team)—GOLD
1996 Trophee Lalique—GOLD
1996 Skate America—GOLD
1996 Continent's Cup—GOLD
1996 Hershey's Kisses Figure Skating Challenge (Team)—GOLD
1996 World Figure Skating Championships—GOLD
1996 ISU Champions Series Finals—GOLD
1996 Centennial On Ice—BRONZE
1996 US Figure Skating Championships—GOLD

1995 US Figure Skating Challenge (Team)—GOLD
1995 Nations Cup—GOLD
1995 Skate Canada—GOLD
1995 Skate America—GOLD
1995 Metropolitan Open (Best Of The Best)—SILVER
1995 Tri-Cities Pro-Am—4th
1995 Spring Pro-Am—GOLD
1995 Worlds—4th
1995 US Nationals—SILVER

1994 Thrifty Challenge—BRONZE
1994 Trophee De France—BRONZE
1994 Skate America—SILVER
1994 US Ladies' Outdoor Challenge—GOLD

1994 Goodwill Games—SILVER
1994 Spring Pro-Am—SILVER
1994 Worlds—8th
1994 US Nationals—SILVER
1994 World Juniors—GOLD

1993 Skate America—7th
1993 Olympic Festival—GOLD
1993 Gardena Spring Trophy—GOLD
1993 US Nationals—6th
1993 Pacific Coast Sectional—GOLD
1993 Southwest Pacific Regional—GOLD

1992 US Nationals (Junior)—9th
1992 Pacific Coast Sectional (Junior)—BRONZE
1992 Southwest Pacific Regional (Junior)—GOLD

Index